I Can Read About™

Bees and Wasps

I Can Read About™

Bees and Wasps

Written by David Cutts • Illustrated by Janice Kinnealy

Consultant: Kathy Carlstead, Ph.D., National Zoological Park, Smithsonian Institution

SCHOLASTIC INC.

New York Toronto London Auckland Sydney
Mexico City New Delhi Hong Kong Buenos Aires

ISBN 0-439-78384-4

12 11 10 9 8 7 6 5 4 3 2 1 6 7 8 9 10 11/0

Printed in China 62

First Scholastic printing, February 2006

What's buzzing in the garden? If you look closely, you may see a bee. Bees are amazing insects. They are so busy!

Can you guess how many kinds of bees there are? There are over twenty thousand different kinds of bees in the world.

There are also thousands of kinds of wasps. Wasps are relatives of bees. Hornets and yellow jackets are two kinds of wasps.

Bees and wasps are insects. Like all insects, they have six legs and their bodies are divided into three parts: the head, the thorax, and the abdomen. And like many insects, bees and most wasps have two pairs of wings. They also have two feelers on their heads called *antennae* (an-TEN-ee).

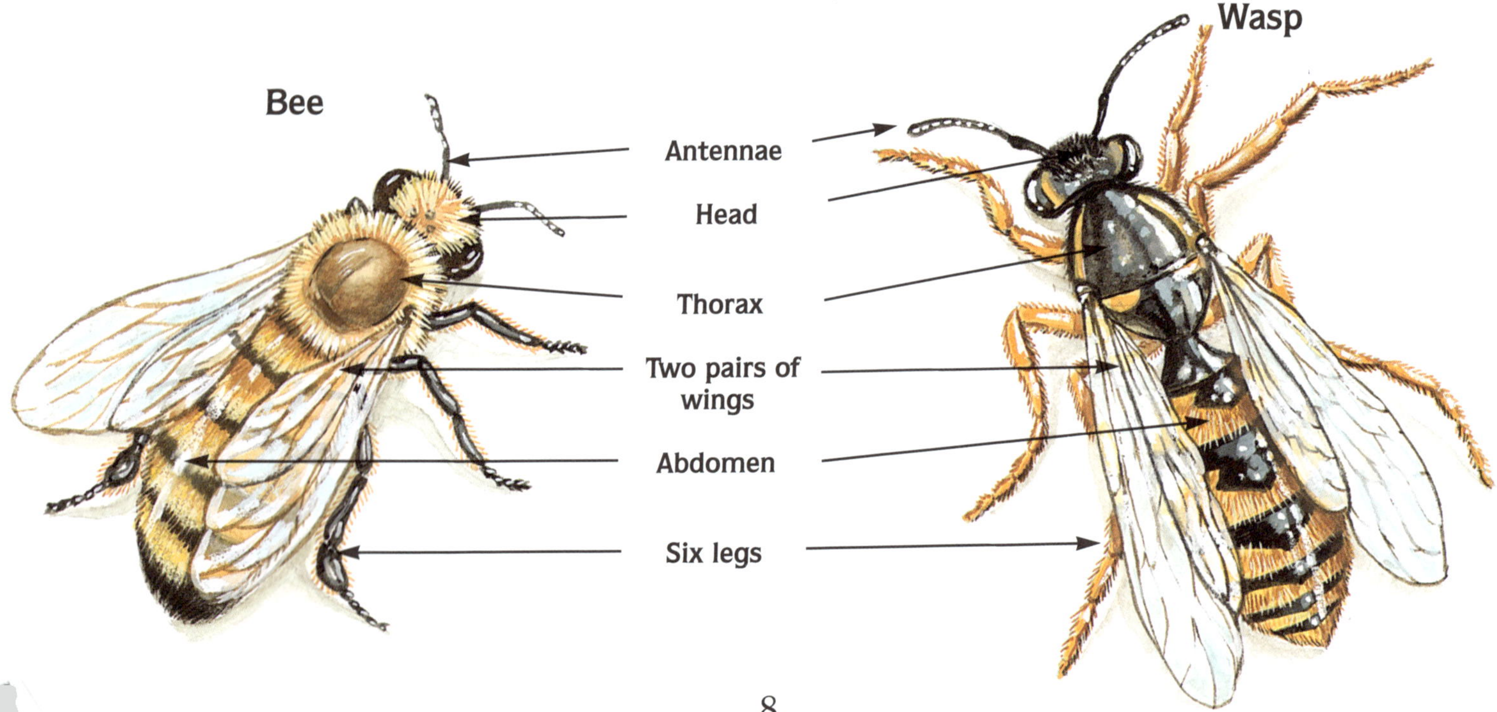

Leafcutting bee is solitary.

Honeybees are social.

Most bees live alone. They are called *solitary* bees. But a few kinds of bees are *social* bees. These bees live in groups called colonies. Social bees work together. They help each other by sharing the chores of the colony.

Honeybees are one kind of social bee. They help each other more than any other kinds of bees.

A colony of honeybees lives in a hive. The hive contains something called a honeycomb. The honeycomb is made of beeswax. Beeswax comes from the wax glands inside the bees' bodies.

Bees often build their hives in trees. But sometimes, they choose a more protected place, such as high up in the rafters of an old barn.

Tens of thousands of honeybees may live in a single hive. But there is only one queen bee in a colony. All the other bees are either workers or drones.

The queen is the only bee in the hive that can lay eggs. That's all she does during spring and summer. A queen honeybee may live for about five years, laying as many as a million eggs during that time.

Most of the other bees in a honeybee colony are workers. Workers are female bees but they cannot lay eggs. They do all the work of the colony, including feeding the young, gathering food, building honeycomb cells, and guarding the colony. Male bees are called drones. They have only one job to do. They mate with the queen or with the queens of other colonies.

Worker gathering food

Workers building honeycomb

Food being passed between workers

Drone

Whether it is part of a natural beehive or a beekeeper's hive, the entrance to a beehive is a busy place. Each day, thousands of workers leave the hive to look for food. They get their food from flowers.

One kind of food honeybees collect is called *pollen.* Workers carry the powdery pollen back to the hive in their *pollen baskets*. Pollen baskets are not really baskets. They are hairs that grow on the bees' back legs. The pollen from flowers sticks to these hairs, making it easy for the bees to carry.

Another kind of food that worker bees collect is called *nectar*. Nectar is a sweet liquid found inside flowers. Bees suck up nectar with their tongues. They carry the nectar back to the hive in their *honey stomachs,* which are located in the bees' abdomens. Then the bees turn the nectar into honey. The honey is used to feed the colony.

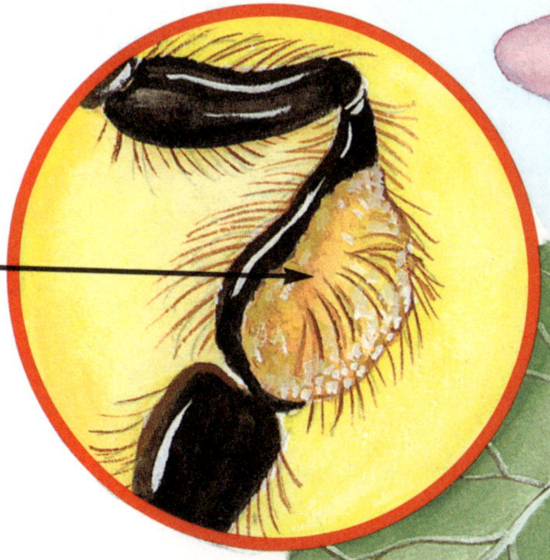

If you could look inside a beehive, you would see a honeycomb made of thousands of tiny "rooms" called cells. The bees build the cells from beeswax. Each cell has six sides. The honeycombs hang from the hive in rows that are back to back.

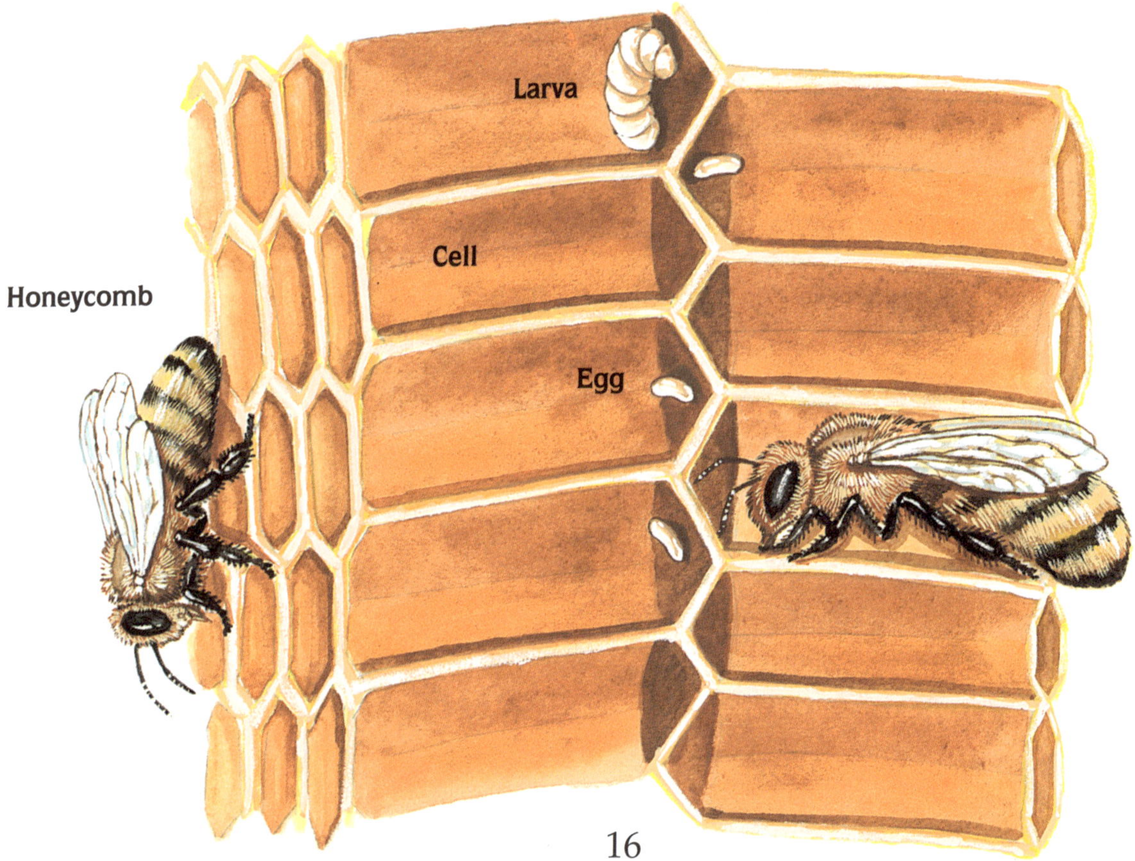

Honeycomb

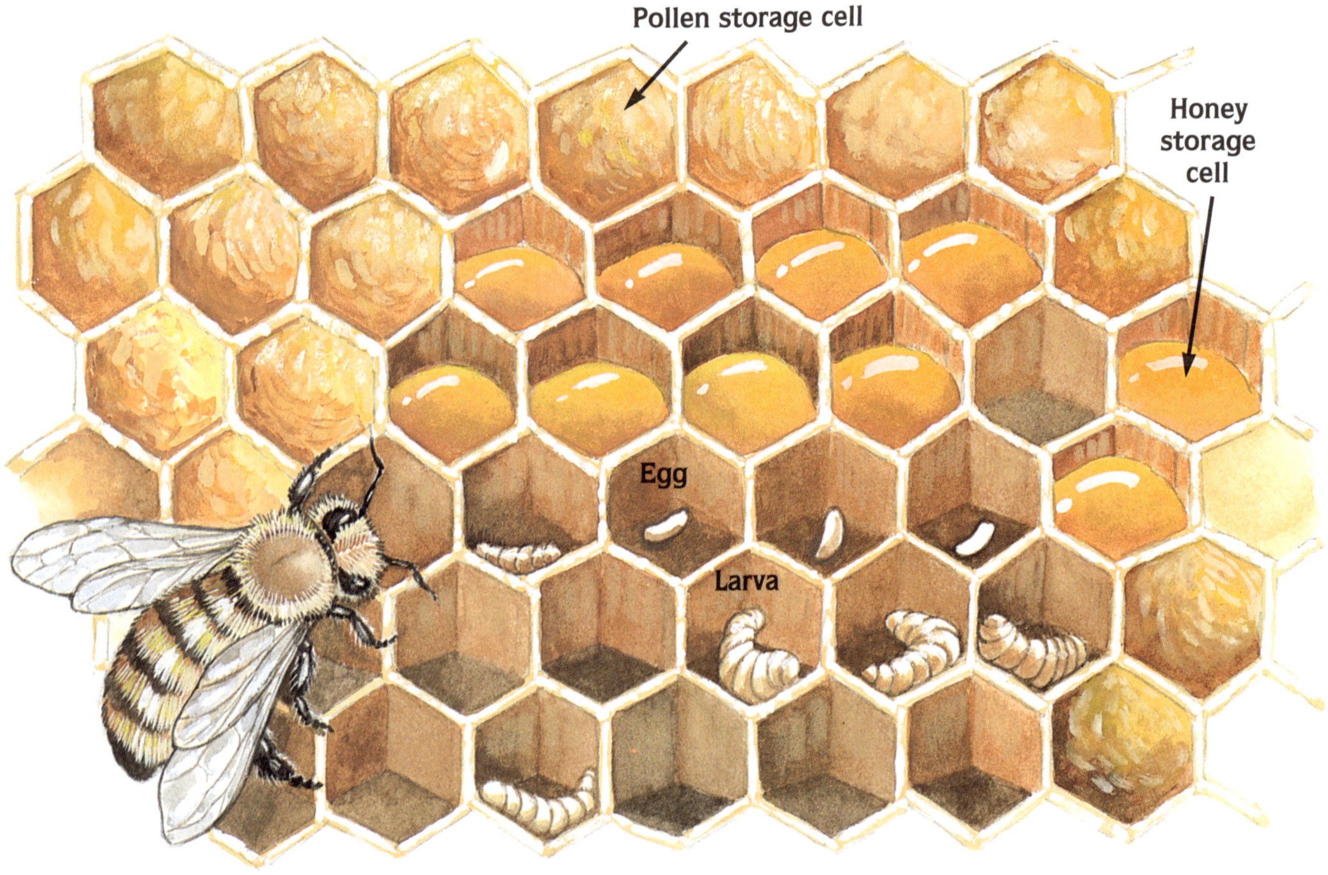

Different cells in the hive are used in different ways. Honey is stored in some. Pollen is stored in others.

Still others are used as a sort of nursery. The queen bee lays one egg in each nursery cell. The eggs are very small—about the size of a pinpoint.

After the queen lays the egg, it takes only three days to hatch. Out crawls a tiny wormlike creature called a *larva* (LAR-vuh).

Worker bees have special glands in their heads. These glands make a food called *royal jelly,* which is full of protein and vitamins.

Worker bees feed royal jelly to the larva for three days. Then, for the next two days, they feed the larva something called *beebread.* Beebread is made of honey and pollen.

Soon the larva spins a silk *cocoon*, or shell. Worker bees use beeswax to close the nursery cell. Inside the cocoon, the larva becomes a *pupa* (PYOO-puh). Finally, about three weeks from the time the egg was laid, out comes a new, fully grown worker bee. It chews its way out of the nursery cell, ready to join in the work of the colony.

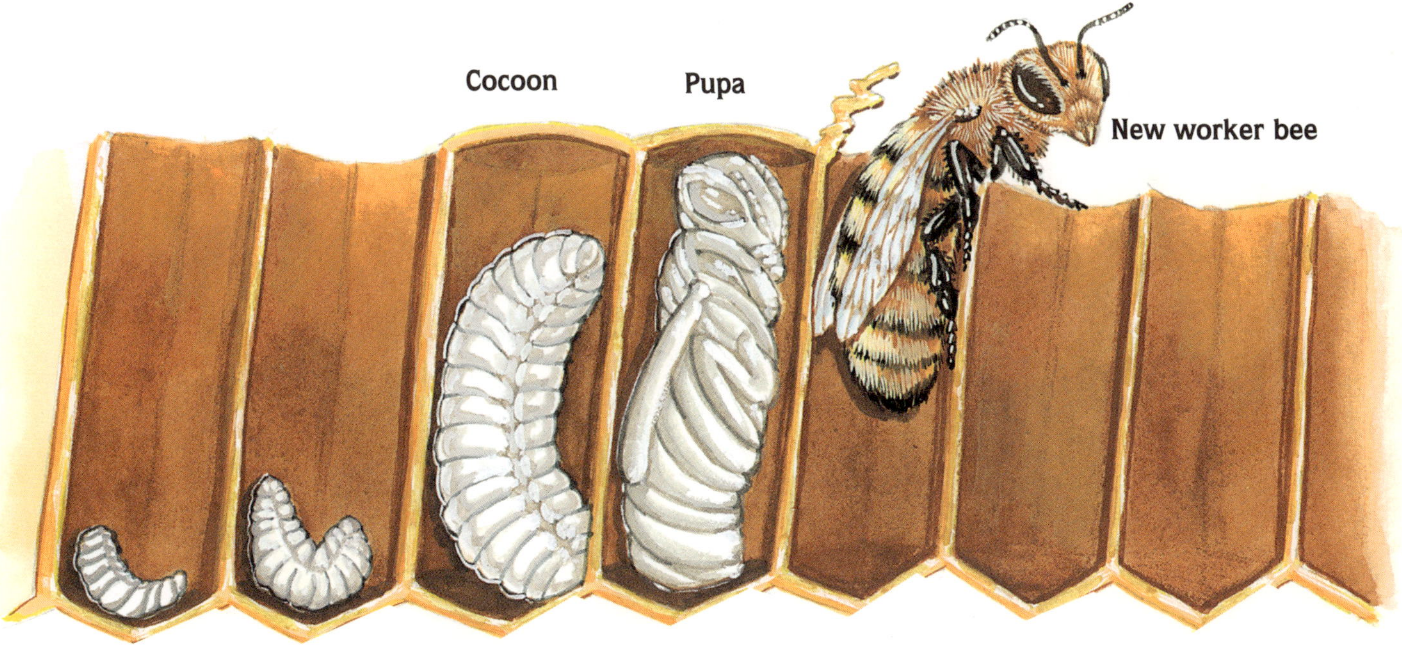

During summer, worker bees live for only five or six weeks. But in that time they have many different jobs. Each job is carried out as the worker reaches a certain age. The youngest workers have jobs in the hive. Older workers are food gatherers.

These pictures show the jobs worker bees perform and the age at which each job is carried out.

Builds cells made of wax (12-15 days old)

Receives and distributes food (16-19 days old)

Guards entrance to hive
(20 days old)

Gathers food for
the colony
(21-42 days old)

When a food gatherer finds food, she shares it with the other bees in the hive. Soon, other food gatherers head for the same food supply. How do they know where to go?

The worker who has found food does a special dance when she gets back to the hive. The kind of dance she does shows the other workers in which direction the food supply is located and how far away it is from the hive.

Worker bees are very busy. As they do their chores, they check on the pollen and honey supplies. They look into the nursery cells. They examine the honeycomb to make sure the hive is large enough. And they keep the queen safe.

Bees have many enemies, including bears, who may ruin a hive while looking for honey to eat. Other creatures, such as skunks, like to eat bees. Worker bees use their venomous stingers to attack such predators.

In the summer, heat can build up inside the hive. Whether it's in the beekeeper's hive or a natural hive, the heat can melt the beeswax cells. So hundreds of worker bees go to the hive's entrance and turn themselves into portable fans. As they fan the air with their wings, they push cool air in and hot air out.

If a queen lays too many eggs, a beehive can get crowded. When this happens, some of the workers leave the hive. The queen goes with them. This is called *swarming*. Scouts look for a good spot for a new colony. When one is found, the workers and queen build a new hive there.

The bees left in the old hive have more room now. At first they don't have a queen. But before long a new queen hatches. Then she and the drones fly out of the hive on a mating flight. Soon the new queen begins laying eggs. And life in the hive goes on.

New queen emerging from cell

Beekeepers are people who raise bees for their delicious, sweet honey and for beeswax. The beeswax is used for candles, polishes, and many other helpful products. Beekeepers' bees build their honeycomb cells on special panels inside wooden hives. The beekeepers can take the panels out to gather the honey and beeswax.

If they move slowly, beekeepers have found that they usually do not get stung by their bees. And as everyone knows, it's wise to avoid being stung by a bee! Among honeybees, only females can sting, and a few hours later, they die.

Bumblebees can sting many times without dying. These large, fuzzy-looking yellow-and-black bees are different from honeybees in other ways, too. Bumblebees are much larger than honeybees, but their colonies are smaller. Instead of building a hive, a queen bumblebee builds a nest on the ground or in the grass.

First, she builds something called a *honey pot* out of wax and fills it with nectar. Next she makes a wax cell for a nest and lays her first eggs in it. These eggs will develop into worker bumblebees. In late summer, the queen and workers will raise new queens and drones. After mating with the drones, the new queens will hibernate during cold weather. In spring, the young queens will begin new colonies.

Bumblebees and honeybees are social bees. But most bees are solitary bees. They live alone. Solitary bees make several different kinds of nests. Carpenter bees drill tunnels into branches or pieces of wood. Each tunnel has several cells, and each cell contains pollen, nectar, and an egg. Wood chips glued together with bee saliva separate the cells.

Leafcutting bees also live in tunnels. These tunnels may be found in branches, in pieces of soft wood, or in the earth. Each tunnel is lined with cells made of leaves and saliva.

Mason bees build their nests out of clay and saliva. The nest may be on a stone, against a wall, or even in a snail shell.

Burrowing bees, or mining bees, dig burrows or tunnels in the earth. Sometimes several bees will share the work of digging one tunnel. But each female bee makes her own private tunnel off the main tunnel, in which she lays an egg.

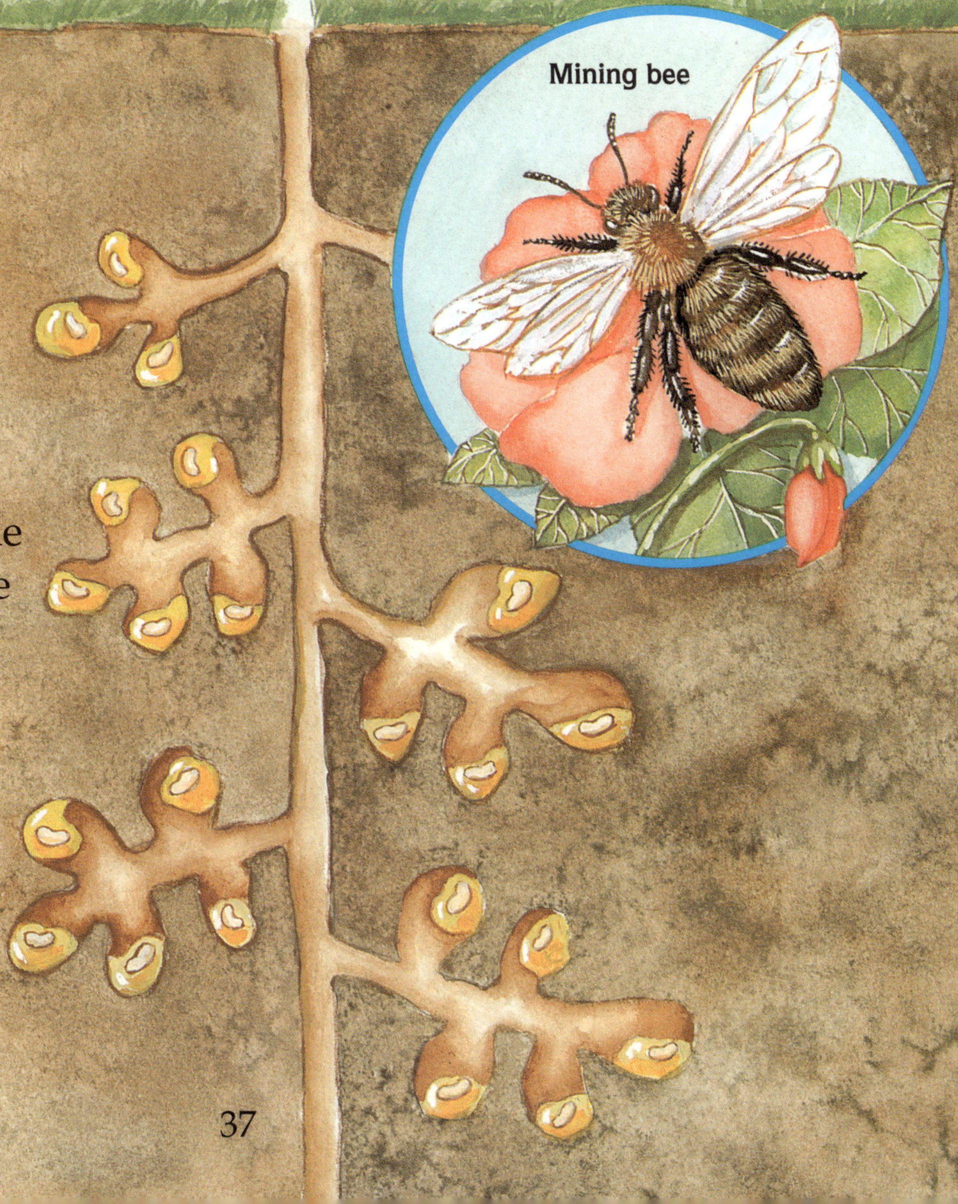

Most female solitary bees die at the end of the summer. But before a female dies, she has a lot to do. In each cell of her nest, she puts some pollen and nectar. Then she lays her eggs in the cells and seals the cells with waterproof wax.

The next spring, the eggs hatch. The young bees are hungry. They eat the food their mother left for them. After that, they are on their own.

Wasps are related to bees. Most wasps lead solitary lives. The female mud dauber is a solitary wasp that makes her nest out of saliva and mud.

Other wasps are social. Social wasps build their nests out of paper. To start a colony, a queen chews plants and wood, then shapes the mixture into separate cells for her eggs. The mixture dries to a papery material. When the eggs hatch into wormlike *larvae* (LAR-vee), or grubs, the queen feeds them insects.

Ten days later, the grubs have turned into worker wasps. The workers collect food and add to the nest as the colony grows.

The queen lays an egg in each of the cells.

Hornets and yellow jackets are social wasps. Yellow jackets may put their nests almost anywhere—in the ground, against a fence, or hanging from a tree.

Hornets often build their nests in trees. But sometimes they choose nesting places that offer more shelter. Some nests are very large and contain thousands of hornets.

Bees and wasps are fascinating insects. And the bee family is also very helpful to people. Honeybees give us honey and wax. Wasps kill many insects that are harmful to humans.

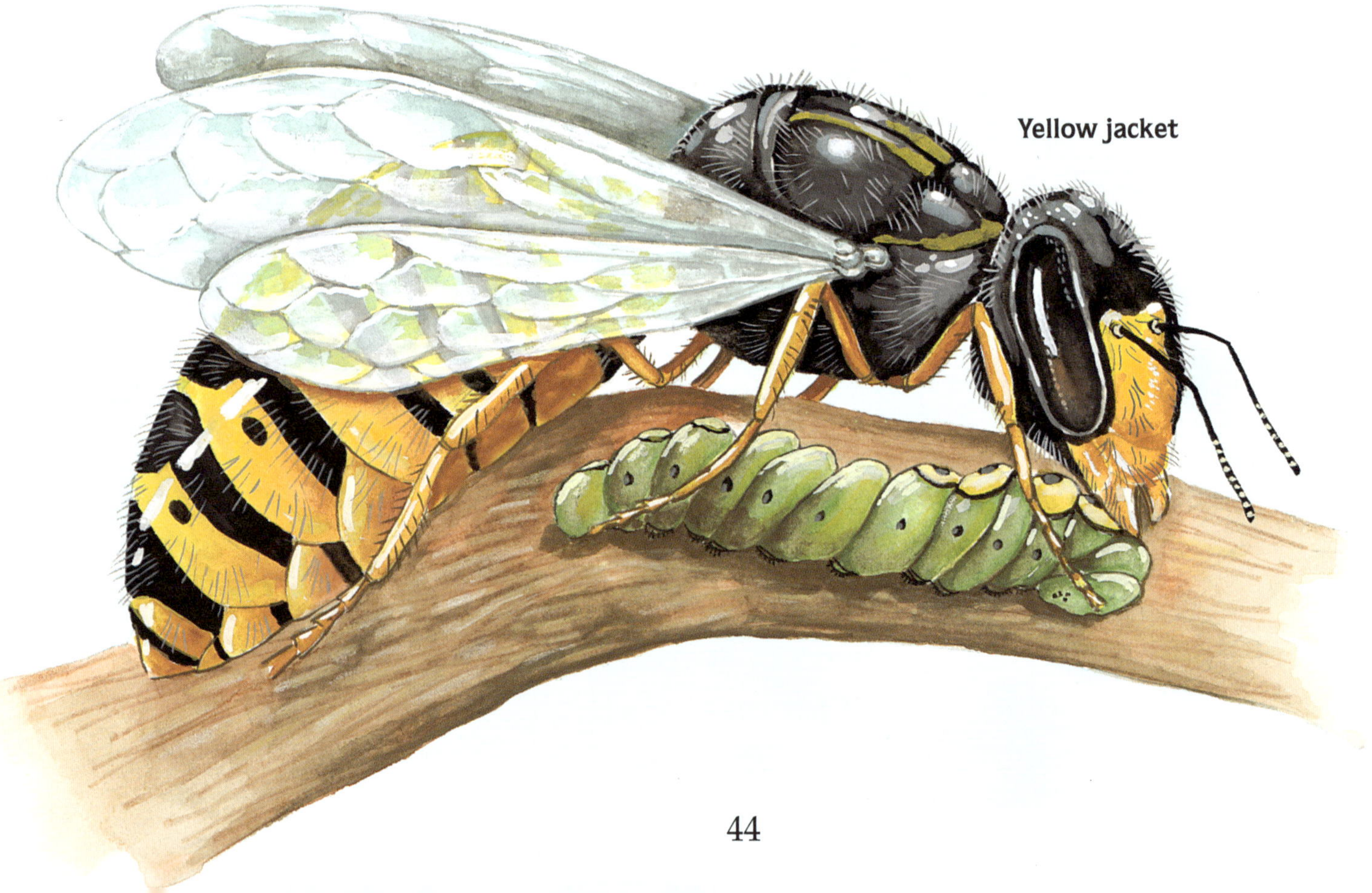

One of the bee's most useful activities takes place when bees carry pollen from flower to flower as they buzz about. The bright colors, sweet smells, and tasty nectar of the flowers attract the bee. When the insect lands on a flower, pollen may stick to its legs. Then, when the bee flies to another flower, some of the pollen may brush off. This helps to pollinate the plants so they can produce fruit and seeds. Many important crops of vegetables and fruits flourish with the help of bees.

So, in a way, plants and bees help each other. Plants give the bees nectar and pollen to eat, and bees help to pollinate the plants.

One summer day, visit a park or garden. Listen for the telltale buzzing of a bee. Then, from a safe distance, stop and watch the bee at work. It is one of the most interesting sights in nature!